I0426212

February 2012

AFGHANISTAN

Improvements Needed to Strengthen Management of U.S. Civilian Presence

G A O
Accountability ★ Integrity ★ Reliability

GAO-12-285

February 2012

AFGHANISTAN

Improvements Needed to Strengthen Management of U.S. Civilian Presence

Why GAO Did This Study

In March 2009, the President called for an expanded U.S. civilian presence under Chief of Mission authority to build the capacity of the Afghan government to provide security, essential services, and economic development. In addition, the Department of Defense (DOD) deploys civilians under combatant commander authority to Afghanistan to support both combat and capacity-building missions. DOD established the Civilian Expeditionary Workforce (CEW) in 2009 to create a cadre of civilians trained, cleared, and equipped to respond urgently to expeditionary requirements. As the military draws down, U.S. civilians will remain crucial to achieving the goal of transferring lead security responsibility to the Afghan government in 2014.

For this report, GAO (1) examined the expansion of the U.S. civilian presence in Afghanistan, (2) evaluated DOD's implementation of its CEW policy, and (3) determined the extent to which U.S. agencies had provided required Afghanistan-specific training to their personnel before deployment. GAO analyzed staffing data and training requirements, and interviewed cognizant officials from the Department of State (State), other U.S. agencies with personnel under Chief of Mission authority in Afghanistan, and DOD.

What GAO Recommends

GAO's recommendations to DOD include developing key assumptions and identifying the number and types of positions that should constitute the CEW, and establishing a process to identify and synchronize training requirements. DOD concurred with GAO's recommendations.

View GAO-12-285. For more information, contact Brenda S. Farrell at (202) 512-3604 or farrellb@gao.gov, or Charles Michael Johnson Jr. at (202) 512-7331 or johnsoncm@gao.gov.

What GAO Found

U.S. agencies under Chief of Mission authority and the Department of Defense (DOD) have reported expanding their civilian presence in Afghanistan and took steps to improve their ability to track that presence. Since January 2009, U.S. agencies under Chief of Mission authority more than tripled their civilian presence from 320 to 1,142. However, although State could report total Chief of Mission numbers by agency, in mid-2011 GAO identified discrepancies in State's data system used to capture more-detailed staffing information such as location and position type. State began taking steps in the fall of 2011 to improve the reliability of its data system. Also, DOD reported expanding its overall civilian presence from 394 civilians in January 2009 to 2,929 in December 2011 to help assist U.S. efforts in Afghanistan. The extent to which DOD's data is reliable is unknown due to omissions and double counting, among other things. In a 2009 report, GAO noted similar data issues and recommended DOD improve data concerning deployed civilians. DOD concurred with the recommendation and expects the issues will be addressed by a new tracking system to be completed in fiscal year 2012.

DOD has taken preliminary steps to implement its Civilian Expeditionary Workforce (CEW) policy, including establishing a program office; however, nearly 3 years after DOD's directive established the CEW, the program has not been fully developed and implemented. Specifically, DOD components have not identified and designated the number and types of positions that should constitute the CEW because guidance for making such determinations has not been provided by the Office of the Secretary of Defense. Officials stated that once key assumptions regarding the size and composition of the CEW have been finalized, implementing guidance will be issued. Until guidance that instructs the components on how to identify and designate the number and types of positions that will constitute the CEW is developed, DOD may not be able to (1) make the CEW a significant portion of the civilian workforce as called for in DOD's fiscal year 2009 Civilian Human Capital Strategic Plan, (2) meet readiness goals for the CEW as required in DOD's Strategic Management Plan for fiscal years 2012-2013, and (3) position itself to respond to future missions.

U.S. agencies under Chief of Mission authority and DOD provided Afghanistan-specific, predeployment training to their civilians, but DOD faced challenges. State offered predeployment training courses to address its requirements for Chief of Mission personnel and designated a centralized point of contact to help ensure that no personnel were deployed without taking required training, including the Foreign Affairs Counter Threat course. While predeployment training requirements were established for Afghanistan by the Office of the Secretary of Defense and the Combatant Commander, DOD relied on its various components to provide the training to its civilians. In some cases, DOD components offered duplicate training courses and did not address all theater requirements in their training because DOD did not have a process for identifying and synchronizing requirements and coordinating efforts to implement them, as called for in the *Strategic Plan for the Next Generation of Training for the Department of Defense*. Absent this process, DOD could not ensure that its civilians were fully prepared for deployment to Afghanistan and that training resources were used efficiently.

_____ United States Government Accountability Office

Contents

Figures

Abbreviations

ACPTS	Afghanistan Civilian Personnel Tracking System
CEW	Civilian Expeditionary Workforce
CONUS	continental United States
DOD	Department of Defense
FACT	Foreign Affairs Counter Threat
HMMWV	High Mobility Multipurpose Wheeled Vehicle
MRAP	Mine Resistant Ambush Protected
State	Department of State
USAID	U.S. Agency for International Development
USDA	U.S. Department of Agriculture

United States Government Accountability Office
Washington, DC 20548

February 27, 2012

Congressional Addressees

In March 2009, the President called for an expanded U.S. civilian presence to build the capacity of the Afghan government to provide security, essential services, and economic development with limited international support. In this expansion, U.S. agencies were to deploy civilian experts under the authority of the Chief of Mission[1] beyond the U.S. Embassy in Kabul to the provinces and districts to create more of an impact on Afghan lives by building the capacity of local government institutions. Housed with military personnel, these field-deployed civilians were to coordinate with their military and Afghan counterparts to integrate their capacity-building activities into the larger counterinsurgency campaign. Additionally, the Department of Defense (DOD) has deployed civilians to Afghanistan under the authority of U.S. Central Command to support combat operations through equipment maintenance, logistical support, and intelligence gathering and analysis. Some DOD civilians also deploy to build the capacity of Afghan security institutions such as the Afghan Ministries of Defense and Interior. DOD established the Civilian Expeditionary Workforce (CEW) by directive in January 2009 to serve as a source for such deployable civilians.[2]

Current U.S. strategy calls for provinces and districts to be transitioned to greater Afghan government control as local capacity improves and conditions allow.[3] The U.S. civilian expansion in Afghanistan and the deployment of those civilians into the field is crucial to these capacity-

---

[1]Chiefs of Mission are the principal officers in charge of U.S. diplomatic missions and have full responsibility for the direction, coordination, and supervision of all government executive branch employees in that country, with some exceptions. The U.S. Ambassador to a foreign country is the Chief of Mission in that country.

[2]Department of Defense Directive 1404.10, *DOD Civilian Expeditionary Workforce* (Jan. 23, 2009).

[3]The U.S. Strategy for Afghanistan refers to the strategy announced in a March 2009 speech by the President and reiterated in a December 2010 strategic review under the auspices of the National Security Council. Planning and implementation of this strategy is further detailed in the August 2009 U.S. Government Integrated Civilian-Military Campaign Plan for Support to Afghanistan and the February 2010 Afghanistan and Pakistan Regional Stabilization Strategy.

building efforts, particularly as the United States, along with its North Atlantic Treaty Organization partners, has committed to fully transferring lead security responsibility to the Afghan government by the end of 2014. Furthermore, a recent report from the Special Inspector General for Afghanistan Reconstruction found that the cost of sustaining the U.S. civilian presence would likely rise as the U.S. military presence decreases.

Because of broad congressional interest in Afghanistan, we performed our work under the authority of the Comptroller General of the United States to conduct work on his own initiative. In this report, we examine issues related to the management of U.S. agency civilian personnel deployed to Afghanistan under both Chief of Mission and DOD authority. Specifically, we (1) examined the expansion of the U.S. civilian presence in Afghanistan, (2) evaluated DOD's implementation of its CEW policy, and (3) determined the extent to which U.S. agencies had provided required Afghanistan-specific training to their personnel before deployment.

For our first objective, to examine the expansion of the U.S. civilian presence in Afghanistan, we obtained and analyzed staffing data from the Department of State (State) and DOD regarding staffing requirements and fill rates for all civilian positions under Chief of Mission authority and key positions under combatant commander authority deployed in-country following the President's March 2009 call to enhance support of Afghan national and subnational government institutions. To determine the reliability of the staffing data, we reviewed available documentation pertaining to the data systems and procedures used to develop staffing data, examined the data for outliers and missing observations, and conducted follow-up interviews to discuss questions that arose in our analysis of the data. Furthermore, we compared State data against staffing data obtained from other agencies under Chief of Mission authority, including the U.S. Agency for International Development (USAID), the U.S. Department of Agriculture (USDA), and the Departments of Homeland Security, Justice, and the Treasury. We found State's staffing data to be sufficiently reliable to provide an indication of the positions filled at the level of the agency but not sufficiently reliable to report on more-detailed staffing information, such as position type. For DOD, we compared program requirements and staffing data for the Ministry of Defense Advisors program and Afghanistan Pakistan Hands program with documentation obtained from the program office. Because DOD staffing data were based on daily submissions from combatant commands, we could not validate its accuracy; however, DOD officials identified the data as sufficiently reliable to illustrate the increase in DOD's overall civilian presence, and we agree.

For our second objective, to evaluate the implementation of DOD's CEW policy, we reviewed relevant documents to identify the structure of the CEW, DOD's plans for implementing the policy, and how the CEW related to departmentwide programs and goals. In addition, we interviewed officials from the Office of the Secretary of Defense, the CEW program office, the military services, and U.S. Central Command to further understand the current status of efforts to fully implement the CEW, the department's plans for the CEW of the future, and how the CEW was currently supporting the department's needs for deployable civilians.

For our third objective, to determine the extent to which U.S. agencies had provided required Afghanistan-specific and Foreign Affairs Counter Threat (FACT)[4] training to their personnel before deployment, we first identified Chief of Mission and DOD training requirements. For personnel under Chief of Mission authority, we compared training requirements with waiver logs, State Foreign Service Institute attendance rosters, available staffing data, and State Diplomatic Security's FACT Tracker to determine whether civilians deploying through the Chief of Mission had received the required training. For DOD, we compared the Office of the Secretary of Defense and U.S. Central Command training requirements[5] with training curricula contained in regulations, training websites, course schedules, and course handbooks offered by DOD organizations that deploy civilians to Afghanistan. In addition, we interviewed relevant officials from agencies under Chief of Mission Authority and DOD. Finally, we observed scenario-based training administered to Chief of Mission and DOD personnel held at the Muscatatuck Urban Training Center in Indiana.

We conducted this performance audit from May 2010 to February 2012 in accordance with generally accepted government auditing standards. Those standards require that we plan and perform the audit to obtain sufficient, appropriate evidence to provide a reasonable basis for our findings and conclusions based on our audit objectives. We believe that the evidence obtained provides a reasonable basis for our findings and conclusions based on our audit objectives. (See app. I for a more complete description of our scope and methodology.)

---

[4]This training addresses threats that U.S. personnel might face in a number of high-threat posts abroad.

[5]Counterinsurgency Qualification Standards and the U.S. Central Command Fragmentary Order 09-1700.

Background

The United States and its international partners from over 40 nations have been engaged in efforts to secure, stabilize, and rebuild Afghanistan since 2001. U.S. civilians have been a vital part of the U.S. strategy. To implement the U.S. strategy, the U.S. Mission Afghanistan committed in April 2009 to expand its civilian personnel both in Kabul and in the field. U.S. government civilians in Afghanistan generally fall under either the authority of the Chief of Mission (i.e., the U.S. Ambassador) or under DOD's combatant commander authority. The Chief of Mission has authority over almost every U.S. executive branch employee there, except those under the command of a U.S. military commander or those on the staff of an international organization.[6] Although typically stationed at the U.S. Embassy and consulates, U.S. Chief of Mission personnel in Afghanistan can also be deployed at a variety of military facilities outside of Kabul. These field-deployed civilians rely on the military for security, mobility, food, and lodging but remain under Chief of Mission authority. The Chief of Mission presence in Afghanistan consists of personnel from several agencies performing a variety of activities, some of which are described in table 1.

---

[6]Executive branch agencies under Chief of Mission authority must obtain Chief of Mission approval before changing the size, composition, or mandate of their staffs and when assigning personnel to the mission or host country, regardless of the duration or purpose of the proposed position or assignment. National Security Decision Directive 38 governs proposals for the establishment of or changes in full-time, permanent, direct-hire positions. We did not gather data on U.S. civilians working for international organizations in Afghanistan.

Table 1: General Activities of U.S. Agencies under Chief of Mission Authority in Afghanistan

U.S. Agency under Chief of Mission authority	General activities
State	Executive management of civilian presence at post and in the field, personnel security, public diplomacy, counternarcotics, capacity building of governance sector, and other technical areas.
USAID	Social sector development, infrastructure, stabilization, democracy and governance, economic growth, and agriculture.
USDA	Agricultural expertise and capacity building of Afghan Ministry of Agriculture, Irrigation, and Livestock.
Department of the Treasury	Mentoring and capacity building of finance-oriented Ministries, as well as attaché function and involvement in the Afghan Threat Finance Cell.
Department of Justice (e.g., Federal Bureau of Investigation and Drug Enforcement Administration)	Combating corruption, disruption, and dismantling of drug trafficking, improving the security of courthouses, and capacity building of justice and governance sectors, as well as of counternarcotics institutions.
Department of Homeland Security (e.g., Customs and Border Protection and Immigration and Customs Enforcement)	Capacity building for border management, security, and customs collection.

Sources: State, USAID, USDA, Department of the Treasury, Department of Justice, and Department of Homeland Security.

In addition, DOD estimates that, since 2001, over 41,000 civilians have deployed worldwide[7] to support combat operations, contingencies, disaster relief, and stability operations, including ongoing operations in Afghanistan. DOD civilians in Afghanistan serve under the authority of the combatant commander responsible for operations in that area of the world—the U.S. Central Command—and support a wide range of DOD missions. These missions include combat support missions that have traditionally been performed by military personnel such as equipment maintenance, logistical support, and intelligence gathering and analysis; noncombat support missions such as administrative positions within the

---

[7]Department of Defense, *Report to Congress: Medical Care for Department of Defense and Non-Department of Defense Federal Civilians Injured or Wounded in Support of Contingency Operations* (Washington, D.C.).

joint task force headquarters; and capacity-building missions parallel to the Chief of Mission effort to improve Afghan security institutions.

To integrate the U.S. civilian expansion into the broader counterinsurgency and stabilization campaign outside of Kabul, the U.S. Mission Afghanistan, U.S. Forces—Afghanistan,[8] and the International Security Assistance Force[9] have established a framework for civilian-military activities. The U.S. and International Security Assistance Force civilian-military effort includes the use of provincial reconstruction teams and district support teams. Provincial reconstruction teams are combined civilian and military groups responsible for integrating the activities of all military and civilian elements in an assigned province. This integration includes harnessing both civilian and military resources to perform security, governance, and development activities to implement the U.S. counterinsurgency and stabilization strategy as well as to monitor and report on progress. District support teams are combined civilian and military groups responsible for integrating the security, governance, and development activities of all civilian and military elements in an assigned district.

To enhance civilian-military coordination, the U.S. Mission Afghanistan has established a parallel civilian structure within each relevant military installation (i.e., regional command down to district support teams), with senior civilian representatives and civilian team leads managing and supervising Mission personnel at each level, as well as coordinating with their military and local Afghan government counterparts. Together, the senior civilians and military commanders at each level coordinate to perform stability, capacity-building, and development operations in their area of responsibility. Mission contingents at the field facilities typically contain State, USAID, and/or USDA personnel. U.S. Drug Enforcement Administration agents also deploy to some military facilities in the field but

[8]U.S. Forces—Afghanistan is the operational arm of DOD in Afghanistan responsible for all missions not covered within the North Atlantic Treaty Organization mandate. The commander of U.S. Forces—Afghanistan also serves as the commander of the North Atlantic Treaty Organization-led International Security Assistance Force.

[9]Since 2001, the United States has worked with international partners under a United Nations mandate to assist Afghanistan in creating a safe and secure environment, in part through the International Security Assistance Force that oversees all coalition military operations in Afghanistan and is organized around six regional commands. U.S. forces in Afghanistan are deployed either as part of the North Atlantic Treaty Organization-led International Security Assistance Force or Operation Enduring Freedom.

primarily conduct counternarcotics activities with U.S. military and Afghan counternarcotics forces.

Chief of Mission and DOD Processes for Fulfilling Civilian Staffing Requirements

U.S. Mission Afghanistan develops requests for Chief of Mission civilian positions in Afghanistan, and State Headquarters approves these requests after consulting with other agencies. In addition, representatives from State, other U.S. agencies under Chief of Mission authority, and U.S. Embassy Kabul participate in periodic interagency staffing reviews. During these staffing reviews, participants use strategic "lines of effort" to classify and prioritize all Chief of Mission positions in Afghanistan according to their priority and feasibility of staffing. Strategic lines of effort for Afghanistan comprise management operations, agriculture, public diplomacy, rule of law, economic growth, counternarcotics, infrastructure, border management, stabilization, governance, threat finance, and bilateral relationship. Approved requirements and their staffing progress are discussed among State, other agencies under Chief of Mission authority such as USAID and USDA, and U.S. Embassy Kabul at biweekly teleconferences. Agencies under Chief of Mission authority rely on both temporary, external hires and permanent employees to staff civilian requirements in Afghanistan. In particular, agencies are relying on special hiring authorities to meet their staffing needs.[10] Figure 1 illustrates how State, USAID, and USDA recruit and identify candidates for positions in Afghanistan.

---

[10]Examples include State "3161 hires" (see 5 U.S.C. § 3161), USAID Foreign Service Limited Appointments (see 22 U.S.C. § 3949), and USDA use of "Schedule B" hiring authority (see 5. C.F.R. § 213.3201).

Figure 1: Staffing Processes Used by State, USAID, and USDA to Recruit and Identify Candidates for Positions in Afghanistan

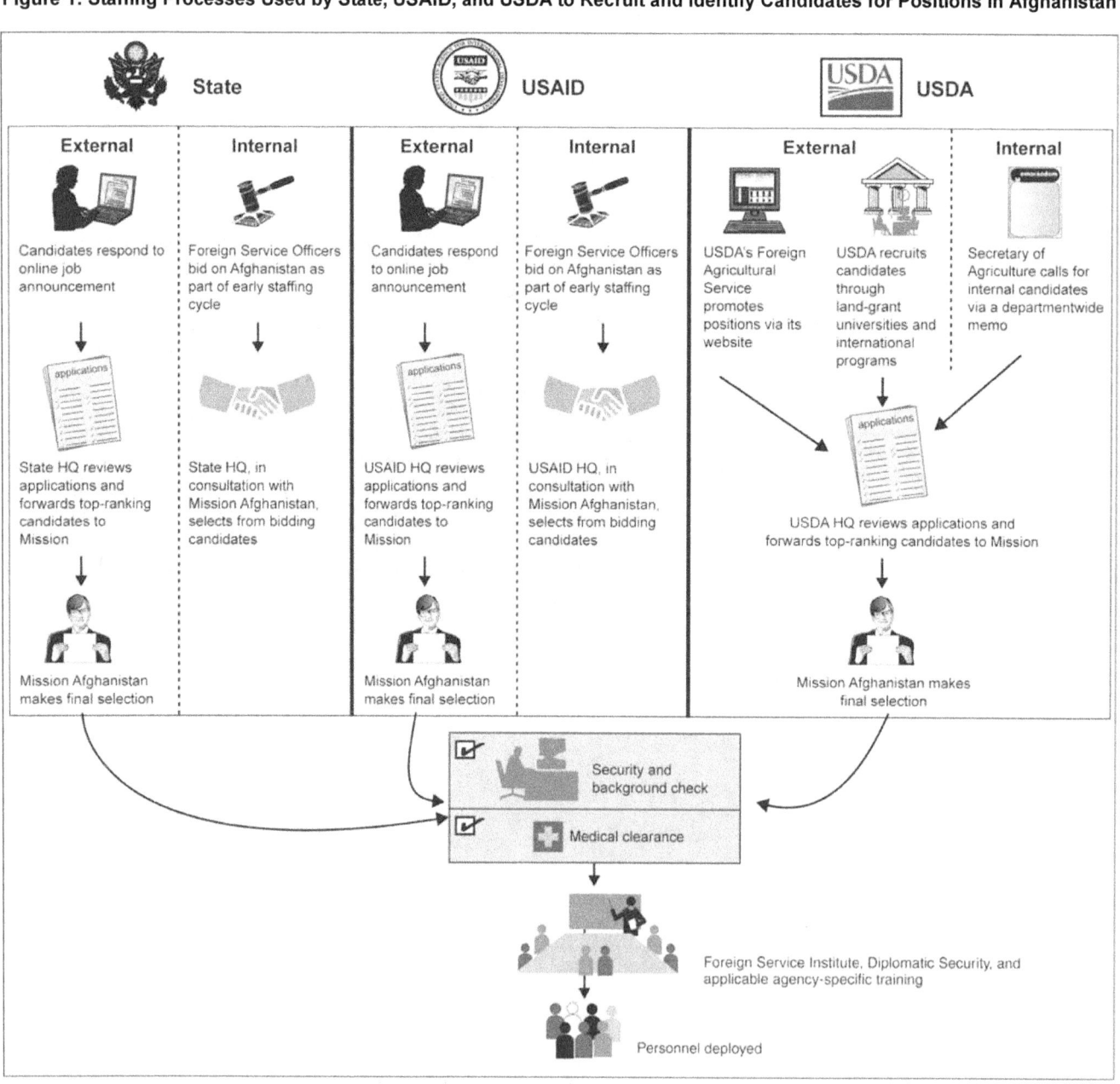

Sources: GAO analysis of State, USAID, and USDA human capital documentation, as well as interviews with agency officials; and Art Explosion (clip art).

GAO-12-285 Afghanistan

DOD relies on an established process for filling civilian positions in Afghanistan. According to DOD officials, the department establishes civilian requirements and fills positions through an integrated military and civilian planning process. Civilian requirements begin at the Joint Task Force level, with commanders identifying military and civilian personnel needed to complete a mission. The commander specifies unit and individual needs in request for forces and joint manning documents, and sends these documents to the corresponding combatant commanders for validation and position designation. When the joint manning document is approved, the Joint Chiefs of Staff record and designate the service responsible for filling positions. At that time, individual positions are designated as military or civilian, or acceptable for either to fill. Once all positions are validated and categorized, the request is sent to the Joint Force Coordinator within the Office of the Joint Chiefs of Staff.[11] A list of individual position requirements is then sent to the services for staffing. Once the staffing source is identified, the requesting commander becomes responsible for tracking which positions have been filled.

To enable the department to readily identify civilians to deploy in support of its missions, including those in Afghanistan, DOD established the CEW program in January 2009 within the Office of the Deputy Assistant Secretary of Defense for Civilian Personnel Policy—which is under the purview of the Under Secretary of Defense for Personnel and Readiness.[12] The CEW is dedicated to creating a cadre of DOD civilians that are organized, ready, trained, cleared, and equipped in a manner that enhances their availability to mobilize and respond urgently to expeditionary requirements now and in the future.

As we previously reported, DOD's use of civilian personnel to support military operations has long raised questions about its policies on compensation and medical benefits for such civilians.[13] Interest in issues

---

[11]This function was previously performed by U.S. Joint Forces Command, which DOD disestablished in August 2011.

[12]Department of Defense Directive 1404.10, *DOD Civilian Expeditionary Workforce* (Jan. 23, 2009).

[13]GAO, *DOD Civilian Personnel: Medical Policies for Deployed DOD Federal Civilians and Associated Compensation for Those Deployed*, GAO-07-1235T (Washington, D.C.: Sept. 18, 2007); and *DOD Civilian Personnel: Greater Oversight and Quality Assurance Needed to Ensure Force Health Protection and Surveillance for Those Deployed*, GAO-06-1085 (Washington, D.C.: Sept. 29, 2006).

related to deployed civilians increased as executive agencies began deploying civilians to support efforts in Iraq and Afghanistan. In 2009, we issued a report that addressed issues related to whether agencies that deployed civilians had (1) comparable policies concerning compensation, (2) comparable policies concerning medical care, and (3) policies and procedures for identifying and tracking deployed civilians. The report contained 18 recommendations made to nine agencies concerning policies related to deployed civilians, including a recommendation to both the Secretary of State and the Secretary of Defense to improve their capability to identify and track deployed civilians. We reported that this capability was critical, so that agencies could notify deployed civilians about emerging health concerns that might affect them.[14]

Chief of Mission and DOD's Training Requirements for Personnel Deploying to Afghanistan

Both Chief of Mission and DOD civilians are to receive Afghanistan-specific training before deployment. According to State, in June 2009 Afghanistan-specific training became mandatory for all Chief of Mission personnel deploying to Afghanistan after October 1, 2009. State's Foreign Service Institute provides this training. In addition to this Afghanistan-specific training, since 2008 State has required that Chief of Mission personnel at high-threat posts such as Afghanistan, Iraq, or Pakistan take the FACT course provided by State's Bureau of Diplomatic Security.[15] This course is designed to address the threats that personnel might face in a number of high-threat posts and includes components on first aid, firearms, counterthreat driving techniques, and duck-and-cover exercises. In addition to these Chief of Mission courses, some U.S. agencies provide their own mission-specific training. Mandatory training requirements for DOD civilians deploying to Afghanistan have been established by the Office of the Secretary of Defense and U.S. Central Command.[16] DOD relies on a variety of organizations—including the Office of the Secretary of Defense and each of the military services—to provide this location-specific training to civilians prior to deployment to Afghanistan. In addition, there are some mission-specific training requirements that

---

[14]GAO, *Human Capital: Actions Needed to Better Track and Provide Timely and Accurate Compensation and Medical Benefits to Deployed Federal Civilians*, GAO-09-562 (Washington D.C.: June 26, 2009).

[15]Some law enforcement and other personnel with specialized training can be waived from this course.

[16]The U.S. Central Command is the combatant command that has operational authority for an area of the globe that consists of 20 countries, including Afghanistan.

civilians must complete. For example, some DOD personnel must complete language and culture training beyond the normal requirement.

U.S. Agencies Reported Expanding Their Civilian Presence in Afghanistan and Took Steps to Improve Their Ability to Track That Presence

Since January 2009, U.S. agencies under Chief of Mission authority more than tripled their civilian presence and expanded outside Kabul in response to the President's 2009 announcement. DOD both created new programs to build the security capacity of the Afghan government and reported expanding its overall civilian presence. U.S. agencies during the course of our review acknowledged data reliability problems with staffing data and have efforts under way to improve the reliability of that data.

U.S. Chief of Mission Presence in Afghanistan More Than Tripled Since 2009

According to State, from January 2009 through December 2011, the Chief of Mission civilian presence more than tripled from 320 to 1,142 civilians, an increase of 257 percent. Overall Chief of Mission staffing requirements also grew during this period from 531 to 1,261 positions, and, as of December 2011, about 91 percent (1,142 of 1,261) of those positions were filled. As of October 2011, State officials did not foresee further expansion of the U.S. civilian presence and planned to change their focus to reconfiguring staffing resources as needed within the existing presence. Figure 2 illustrates the increased U.S. Chief of Mission presence in Afghanistan since January 2009.

Figure 2: Increase in U.S. Chief of Mission Presence in Afghanistan, January 2009 through December 2011

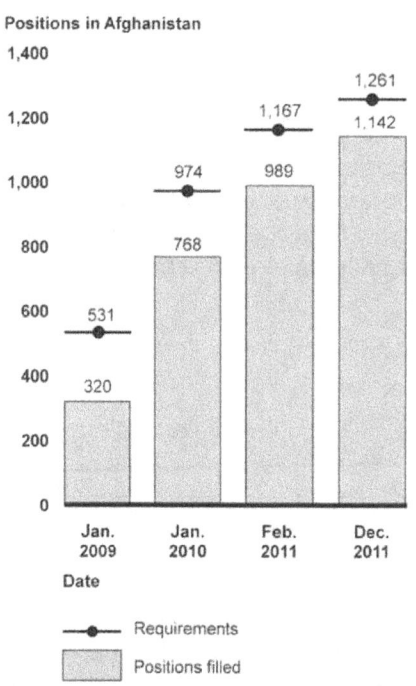

Positions in Afghanistan

Date

- Requirements
- Positions filled

Source: State Department Chief of Mission Civilian Staffing Matrix.

Note: According to State officials, U.S. Embassy Kabul also utilized "other Chief of Mission civilians"—i.e., short-term deployments, key contractors, and elig ble family members—to temporarily fill some high-priority staffing gaps. Temporary staff totals included 137 for January 2010, 135 for February 2011, and 97 for December 2011. State could not provide data on other Chief of Mission civilians for January 2009. We could not verify the extent to which these temporary staff substituted for official approved positions.

Of the nine executive branch agencies under Chief of Mission authority, as of December 2011 State, USAID, Department of Justice, and USDA had filled most of the Chief of Mission position requirements, as illustrated in table 2.

Table 2: Extent to Which Agencies Had Filled Chief of Mission Staffing Requirements in Afghanistan, December 2011

Agency	Position requirements	Positions filled	Percentage of position requirements filled
Mission	1,261	1,142	90.6
Kabul	732	686	93.7
Field	529	456	86.2
State	594	577	97.1
USAID	378	366	96.8
Department of Justice	154	116	75.3
USDA	77	55	71.4
Department of Homeland Security	25	23	92.0
Department of the Treasury[a]	16	11	68.8
Department of Transportation	15	12	80.0
Health and Human Services	1	1	100.0
Department of Commerce	1	1	100.0

Source: State Department Chief of Mission Civilian Staffing Matrix.

Notes: These numbers reflect State data on requirements and filled positions as of December 6, 2011, and do not reflect any changes that have occurred since that time.

[a]The Department of the Treasury noted that State's database had not been updated to reflect 13 total approved Treasury positions. Treasury further noted that two of its positions listed as "open" remained programmatically on hold, resulting in 11 active slots filled.

Additionally, the Chief of Mission presence expanded outside Kabul—a response to the President's call for greater U.S. civilian expertise at provincial and district levels. From January 2009 through December 2011, field position requirements grew by approximately 260 percent (from 147 to 529), and over 85 percent of those requirements were filled. These positions are assigned to locations throughout Afghanistan, including at military facilities such as provincial reconstruction and district support teams and at State's regional consulates.

Comparing the Chief of Mission Civilian Staffing Matrix[17] numbers with the position requirements reported by individual agencies, we found that the data in the Chief of Mission Civilian Staffing Matrix were sufficiently reliable for identifying high-level staffing information such as total number of positions filled by each agency under Chief of Mission authority. According to State officials, the high-level staffing data identified in the Chief of Mission Civilian Staffing Matrix are updated weekly using data from U.S. agencies and are also validated through periodic teleconferences, including staff from State headquarters, other agencies, and the U.S. Embassy in Kabul.

State Took Steps to Enhance Its Ability to Track Its Civilian Presence

The 2010 Afghanistan and Pakistan Regional Stabilization Strategy emphasizes the need to match civilian personnel's expertise to specific mission requirements on the ground. Furthermore, according to federal internal control standards, program managers need operational data to determine whether they are meeting the goals of their agencies' strategic and annual performance plans and accounting for the effective and efficient use of resources.[18] U.S. Embassy Kabul and State's Office of Orientation and In-Processing (responsible for ensuring that interagency personnel meet all administrative, medical, and training requirements before deploying to Afghanistan) began using a data system called the Afghanistan Civilian Personnel Tracking System (ACPTS) in February 2011 to track Chief of Mission personnel's locations and movements (e.g., movement from Kabul to a district support team) and to identify position-specific information (e.g., location, position title, appointment type or grade, vacancy status, and the strategic line of effort to which a position belongs). State officials noted that they planned to use this information to optimize the U.S. presence in the next interagency staffing exercise, when they might need to be prepared to reconfigure the existing presence. However, when we examined this data system in March and July 2011, we found discrepancies that called into question the system's reliability. For example, the ACPTS data we received were insufficiently reliable to determine which strategic line of effort contained the greatest staffing shortfall—crucial information for an interagency staffing exercise.

---

[17]According to State officials, this matrix serves as the authoritative record on Chief of Mission staffing requirements and positions filled in Afghanistan.

[18]GAO, *Standards for Internal Control in the Federal Government*, GAO/AIMD-00-21.3.1 (Washington D.C.: November 1999).

Over 60 percent of the ACPTS records for July 2011 (648 of 1,192) were missing data in at least 1 of 10 data fields. Our analysis revealed, for example, that 36 percent of the appointment grade fields and 30 percent of the line-of-effort fields were missing. We also found discrepancies between the ACPTS and Chief of Mission Civilian Staffing Matrix with regard to the overall position requirements and the number of positions filled. Table 3 lists the discrepancies we identified in State, USAID, and USDA totals.

Table 3: Discrepancies between Chief of Mission Civilian Staffing Matrix and ACPTS

Chief of Mission agency		Position requirements			Positions filled		
		Chief of Mission Civilian Staffing Matrix	ACPTS	Delta	Chief of Mission Civilian Staffing Matrix	ACPTS	Delta
State	Kabul	385	384	-1	360	317	-43
	Field	204	177	-27	149	134	-15
USAID	Kabul	161	181	20	148	167	19
	Field	217	198	-19	153	179	26
USDA	Kabul	17	19	2	10	10	0
	Field	60	61	1	44	33	-11

Source: GAO analysis of State Chief of Mission Civilian Staffing Matrix (June 28, 2011) and ACPTS (July 7, 2011) datasets.

Our discussions with State, USAID, and USDA officials revealed additional discrepancies in the ACPTS data, including duplicate entries, position titles that did not match official position documentation, and inaccurate arrival dates and appointment grade information.

In June 2011, State officials acknowledged that these challenges prevented ACPTS from being used effectively to aggregate detailed, position-specific information regarding the overall U.S. civilian presence in Afghanistan. Although we could not verify the accuracy of the ACPTS system, during the course of our review and after several discussions with us regarding data reliability, in the fall of 2011 State began taking steps to improve the reliability of the ACPTS database. For example, according to State officials, the Office of Orientation and In-Processing recently completed a review of the ACPTS system that included correcting inaccuracies, revising data fields to better reflect actual information being entered, and deleting unnecessary data fields. State has also established standard operating procedures for updating the ACPTS system. For example, according to State officials, the U.S. Embassy's Arrivals and Departure Unit will be responsible for completing the ACPTS records of newly deployed staff once they arrive in-country, and the Interagency

Provincial Affairs Office will be responsible for updating their location information if their duty station changes in the field. Furthermore, in October 2011, U.S. Embassy Kabul issued a new policy for Mission staffing and accountability that established a notification and reporting system to conduct accountability checks of Chief of Mission staff and also outlined the responsibilities of supervisors and individuals in ensuring staffing accountability and tracking. According to State officials, Embassy Kabul conducts monthly data calls with all agencies present in Kabul in accordance with this policy, and the collected data is reconciled with ACPTS data.

DOD Reported Expanding Its Civilian Presence in Afghanistan

According to the Joint Chiefs of Staff's Joint Personnel Status Report, DOD increased its overall civilian presence in Afghanistan by approximately 643 percent from January 2009 through December 2011. While officials acknowledged that some inaccuracies existed in the data provided by this report, they believed that the data fairly depict the increase in the overall DOD civilian presence in Afghanistan. As shown in figure 3, DOD reported its civilian presence in Afghanistan grew from 394 civilians in January 2009 to 2,929 in December 2011.

Figure 3: Reported Increase in DOD Overall Civilian Presence in Afghanistan, January 2009 through December 2011

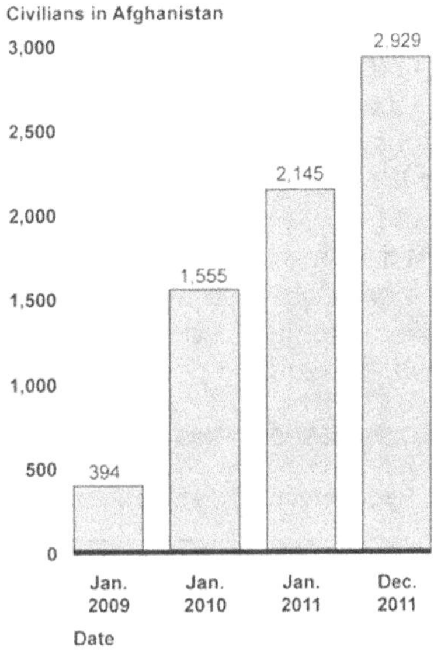

Civilians in Afghanistan

Date	Civilians
Jan. 2009	394
Jan. 2010	1,555
Jan. 2011	2,145
Dec. 2011	2,929

Source: Joint Chiefs of Staff Joint Personnel Status Report

Note: We could not validate the accuracy of the data provided by the Joint Personnel Status Report. DOD officials believe the data are sufficiently accurate to illustrate the increase in the civilian presence in Afghanistan, and we agree.

These civilians serve in a variety of roles that support both DOD's combat mission and its capacity-building efforts. However, it is difficult to specify the number of civilians within DOD's overall civilian presence that supported the capacity-building efforts because these civilians frequently fill positions that support both combat support and capacity-building missions. For example, civilians that deploy with the U.S. Army Corps of Engineers support multiple projects involving both Afghan National Security Forces and U.S. military forces, making it difficult to identify the number of civilians that support capacity-building efforts.

In addition, DOD established two programs to respond to the department's mission to build the capacity of the Afghan government. The first program—Ministry of Defense Advisors, created in fiscal year 2010—operates under the authority of the Under Secretary of Defense for Policy and deploys senior DOD civilians for up to 2 years to serve as advisors to officials in the Afghan government's Ministries of Defense and Interior to exchange knowledge concerning defense-related issues. The Ministry of Defense Advisor program was designed to forge long-term relationships that strengthen Afghanistan's security institutions.[19] The second program—Afghanistan Pakistan Hands, created in fiscal year 2009—operates under the authority of the Joint Chiefs of Staff and deploys DOD civilians for 5 years to serve as experts on Afghanistan and Pakistan to support the counterinsurgency strategy. Specifically, these civilians engage directly with host country officials to enhance government, interagency, and multinational cooperation and fill related positions outside the region. As of December 2011, these programs had identified requirements for 156 civilian positions, and 106 of these positions were filled. At the time of our review, officials were unclear as to whether the requirements for these two programs would stabilize, increase, or decrease. In table 4, we show the extent to which each of these programs had filled the required positions.

Table 4: Extent to Which DOD's New Capacity-Building Programs Had Filled Staffing Requirements in Afghanistan, as of December 2011

Program	Position requirements	Positions filled	Percentage of positions filled
Ministry of Defense Advisor program	102	60[a]	59
Afghanistan Pakistan Hands program	54	46	85
Total	**156**	**106**	**68**

Source: Offices of Ministry of Defense Advisor and Afghanistan Pakistan Hands programs.

[a]Program officials indicated that an additional 11 advisors had been selected to fill positions in Afghanistan and would begin training in January 2012 for deployment in March 2012. Ministry of Defense Advisor program officials indicated, however, that the number of candidates scheduled to begin training was likely to change prior to the beginning of training.

DOD Took Steps to Improve Its Ability to Track Its Civilian Presence

Although DOD has aggregate staffing data for deployed civilians within a country or geographical region, its current data system for tracking deployed civilians may not provide sufficiently reliable information to characterize the specific location and identity of deployed civilians within a country. DOD uses the Joint Personnel Status Report to track the number and location of military, civilian, and contractor personnel

---

[19]For more information on DOD's capacity-building efforts at the Afghan Ministries of Defense and Interior, see GAO, *Afghanistan: Actions Needed to Improve Accountability of U.S. Assistance to Afghanistan Government*, GAO-11-710 (Washington D.C.: July 20, 2011).

deployed worldwide. This report is manually created each day by the combatant commands to include the number and location of personnel within their area of responsibility.[20] However, Joint Chiefs of Staff officials told us that the system contains inaccuracies. For example, the officials noted previous reports have omitted and double counted some personnel, as well as listed some personnel in the wrong locations. The officials stated they could not quantify the magnitude of these inaccuracies due to the system's reliance on manual updates from the individual combatant commands and limited demographic data. We reported in 2009 that DOD issued guidance and established procedures for identifying and tracking deployed civilians in 2006 but concluded in 2008 that its guidance and procedures were not being consistently implemented across the department. In 2009, we found that these policies were still not being fully implemented and recommended that DOD establish mechanisms to ensure that these policies were implemented.[21] In response to this recommendation, DOD stated that it would work with the Defense Manpower Data Center to develop a tracking system for deployed civilians and hoped to have the system completed by September 2009.

At the time of our review, Joint Staff officials stated that in conjunction with the Defense Manpower Data Center, they had completed development and were fielding this automated tracking system that would access information from service specific personnel databases in conjunction with Common Access Card usage in theater to establish and record the specific location of employees.[22] According to DOD officials, this new system will provide DOD with an automated system to track the

---

[20]DOD defines a combatant command as a unified or specified command with a broad continuing mission under a single commander that typically has geographic or functional responsibilities. Geographical commands include U.S. Africa Command, U.S. Central Command, U.S. European Command, U.S. Northern Command, U.S. Pacific Command, and U.S. Southern Command. Functional commands include U.S. Special Operations Command, U.S. Strategic Command, and U.S. Transportation Command.

[21]GAO, *Human Capital: Actions Needed to Better Track and Provide Timely and Accurate Compensation and Medical Benefits to Deployed Federal Civilians,* GAO-09-562 (Washington D.C.: June 26, 2009). This report examined a number of issues concerning deployed civilians, including compensation and benefits; medical care during and following deployment; and the ability of agencies to track the number and location of their deployed civilians.

[22]The Common Access Card is the standard identification badge for all DOD personnel, including military, reserve, guard, civilian, and contractors. The card is typically used to enter military installations.

number, identity, and location of deployed civilians. As we reported in both 2005 and 2009, this type of information is critical for identifying potential exposures or other incidents related to a civilian's deployment.[23] DOD officials stated that, once operational within a combatant commander's area of responsibility, this system will automatically create a report that fulfills Joint Personnel Status reporting requirements for identifying the number and location of military, civilian, and contractor personnel deployed globally. However, according to Joint Chiefs of Staff officials, this system will not be ready to support these reporting requirements within the Central Command area of responsibility until the middle of fiscal year 2012.

DOD Took Preliminary Steps to Implement CEW Policy but Did Not Identify the Number and Types of Positions That Should Constitute the CEW

The Office of the Secretary of Defense for Personnel and Readiness is responsible for overseeing implementation of the 2009 CEW directive, including developing policy and implementing procedural guidance for the CEW. To implement the policies in this directive, the heads of the DOD components are to identify and designate positions as emergency-essential, non-combat essential, and capability-based volunteers as part of the CEW.[24] Emergency-essential positions are those that support the success of combat operations or the availability of combat-essential systems. Non-combat essential positions support the expeditionary requirements in other than combat or combat support situations. Capability-based volunteers are employees who may be asked to volunteer for deployment, to remain behind after other civilians have evacuated, or to fill the positions of other DOD civilians who have deployed to meet expeditionary requirements in order to ensure that critical expeditionary requirements are fulfilled.[25] Finally, according to the directive, the components are to plan, program, and budget for CEW requirements.

---

[23]GAO-09-562 and GAO, *Defense Health Care: Improvements Needed in Occupational and Environmental Health Surveillance during Deployments to Address Immediate and Long-Term Health Issues,* GAO-05-632 (Washington, D.C.: July 14, 2005).

[24]DOD officials noted that separate from the CEW, DOD components have some civilian positions designated as "emergency-essential" and deploy those personnel to support their specific missions.

[25]Department of Defense Directive 1404.10, *DOD Civilian Expeditionary Workforce* (Jan. 23, 2009).

We found that DOD had taken preliminary steps to implement the CEW. Specifically, DOD had (1) established a CEW program office, (2) created a database containing resumes submitted by volunteers, (3) advertised expeditionary positions for civilians on a designated website, and (4) established predeployment training requirements for volunteers selected to fill CEW positions.[26] According to CEW officials, approximately 10 percent to 15 percent of the 2,929 filled civilian positions in Afghanistan were filled by CEW volunteers and the remaining positions were primarily filled by civilian personnel in the military services and other DOD components.

However, the CEW program has not been fully developed and implemented. In particular, DOD components have not identified and designated the number and types of positions that should constitute the emergency-essential, non-combat essential, and capability-based volunteer segments of the CEW because guidance for making such determinations has not been provided by the Office of the Secretary of Defense. Office of the Secretary of Defense officials stated that once key assumptions regarding the size and composition of the CEW have been finalized, implementing guidance will be issued that will contain information on how the components are to identify and designate positions as emergency-essential, non-combat essential and capability-based volunteers. However, Office of the Secretary of Defense officials were not sure as to when this guidance would be issued.[27]

By not developing guidance that instructs the components on how to identify and designate the number and types of positions that will constitute the CEW, DOD may not be able to (1) make the CEW a significant portion of the civilian workforce as called for in DOD's Fiscal Year 2009 Civilian Human Capital Strategic Plan,[28] (2) meet readiness goals for the CEW as required in DOD's Strategic Management Plan for

---

[26]Training requirements included generic training applicable to all CEW selectees as well as location-specific training.

[27]Office of the Secretary of Defense officials first indicated in June 2011 that this draft guidance was being coordinated, but the final guidance has not yet been finalized and issued.

[28]Department of Defense, *Report on the Strategic Human Capital Plan for Civilian Employees of the Department of Defense 2006-2010.*

Fiscal Years 2012-2013,[29] and (3) position itself to respond to future missions.

First, in DOD's fiscal year 2009 civilian human capital strategic plan, DOD identified the CEW as a significant segment of the overall DOD civilian workforce dedicated to supporting DOD operations, contingencies, emergencies, humanitarian missions, stability and reconstruction operations, and combat missions. Further, this plan noted the importance of conducting a gap analysis[30] to identify any differences between the current civilian workforce and the workforce that will be needed in the future for each of the department's "mission critical occupations"—i.e., occupations that are essential to carrying out the department's mission.[31] In July 2011, we testified that identifying skills and capability gaps of the civilian workforce is critical for DOD's strategic planning efforts and that DOD should conduct gap analyses to identify gaps in both the current and the future workforces.[32] Completing a gap analysis is important for DOD to develop strategies to acquire and retain the needed workforce. Further, once workforce needs and strategies are identified, the DOD components will be better positioned to plan, program, and budget for CEW requirements as called for in the CEW directive.

Second, as called for by the Department of Defense Strategic Management Plan for Fiscal Years 2012-2013, DOD's goal to get the right workforce mix should occur through several initiatives, including one to improve the readiness of the CEW by increasing the percentage of

---

[29]Department of Defense Strategic Management Plan FY 2012-2013 (Sept. 20, 2011).

[30]Our body of work has consistently defined a workforce gap analysis to include gaps in critical skills and competencies. See GAO, *Human Capital: Opportunities Exist to Build on Recent Progress to Strengthen DOD's Civilian Human Capital Strategic Plan*, GAO-09-235 (Washington, D.C.: Feb. 10, 2009); *DOD Civilian Personnel: Comprehensive Strategic Workforce Plans Needed*, GAO-04-753 (Washington, D.C.: June 30, 2004); *Human Capital: A Guide for Assessing Strategic Training and Development Efforts in the Federal Government*, GAO-03-893G (Washington, D.C.: July 2003); and *A Model of Strategic Human Capital Management*, GAO-02-373SP (Washington, D.C.: Mar. 15, 2002).

[31]DOD's civilian human capital strategic plan is published by the Under Secretary of Defense for Personnel and Readiness.

[32]GAO, *DOD Civilian Personnel: Competency Gap Analyses and Other Actions Needed to Enhance DOD's Strategic Workforce Plans*, GAO-11-827T (Washington, D.C.: July 14, 2011).

GAO-12-285 Afghanistan

emergency-essential and non-combat essential personnel who are qualified as ready. However, without an understanding of the number and types of positions in the emergency-essential and non-combat essential categories, the current CEW is not positioned to support this DOD priority.

Third, DOD officials told us that institutionalizing the CEW is critical to DOD efforts to best utilize its total workforce structure—military, civilian, and contractor personnel—because the difficulties associated with identifying and deploying civilians are not unique to the ongoing operations in Afghanistan. According to DOD officials, similar issues were experienced in Bosnia, but because the organization and processes that supported the deployment of civilians during that operation were not retained, DOD had to reconstitute the capability to identify and deploy civilians when the need arose for civilians to deploy to Iraq and Afghanistan.

U.S. Agencies Established Afghanistan-Specific Predeployment Training Requirements, but DOD Faced Implementation Challenges

State Provided Required Training for Personnel Deploying to Afghanistan

State has established predeployment training requirements for all Chief of Mission personnel deploying to Afghanistan, including courses offered by State's Foreign Service Institute, as well as key security training provided by State's Diplomatic Security Bureau—the FACT course. The Foreign Service Institute's Afghanistan-specific training courses address State's 2009 training requirement for Chief of Mission personnel deploying to Afghanistan and focus on providing Chief of Mission personnel with basic professional skills and knowledge needed to participate in stabilization and reconstruction activities as members of the U.S. Embassy Kabul or its subordinate entities. Additionally, the training recognizes the requirements for effectively operating in a complex environment, including administrative, survival, and day-to-day functioning/life support. Table 5 further describes the Foreign Service Institute's training for Chief of Mission personnel.

Table 5: State-Required, Afghanistan-Specific Training for Chief of Mission Personnel

	Afghanistan Familiarization	Afghanistan Field Orientation	Interagency Civilian-Military Integration Training Exercise
Course description	Overview of • Afghanistan's history, culture, and politics, including counterinsurgency and border issues; • U.S. political and military strategy in Afghanistan; and • U.S. agency programs in Afghanistan. • Specific topics include threat assessments, counterintelligence awareness, and deployment-related administrative and logistic information.	For personnel assigned to provincial reconstruction teams: • Basic professional skills and knowledge essential for functioning as a member of a civilian-military field team. • Training on dealing with traumatic events, Afghan tribal dynamics and Taliban tactics, integration of civilian-military planning, and tools for assessing district stability.	Applying lessons learned from the Afghanistan Field Orientation course in a simulated environment by working with military colleagues, • learning security procedures for travel by military convoy or helicopter, and • using interpreters during scripted training events featuring Afghan role-players. • Scenarios include simulations of insurgent attacks.

Source: GAO summary of Foreign Service Institute's course catalog and materials for fiscal year 2011.

All Chief of Mission personnel are required to take the Afghanistan Familiarization course, while all personnel deploying to locations outside of Kabul are also required to take the Afghanistan Field Orientation and the Interagency Civilian-Military Integration Training Exercise courses. According to State officials, the Afghanistan Familiarization course covers subjects that contribute to employees' success on the job, such as orientation issues and State support at high-threat posts. Additionally, the Afghanistan Field Orientation course covers subjects that State has identified as needed for the success of provincial reconstruction teams and other civilian-military entities at the regional and district levels. According to State and contractor officials we interviewed during our observation of the Interagency Civilian-Military Integration Training Exercise at the Muscatatuck Urban Training Center in Butlerville, Indiana, personnel who attend this training are able to practice working in situations they would likely encounter while deployed. The training includes working through an interpreter and heavily interacting with Afghan officials. In addition, because field-deployed civilians live and work alongside military colleagues, the exercises focus on the cultural (e.g., education about military ranks) and practical (e.g., participation in convoy security) aspects of working with the military, as shown in figure 4.

Figure 4: Trainees React to Simulated Mortar Attack during Interagency Civilian-Military Integration Training Exercise

Source: GAO

Civilian-military training exercise.

During the Interagency Civilian-Military Integration Training Exercise, students get the opportunity to simulate living with the military on a Forward Operating Base, and travel by convoy and helicopter to meetings with their Afghan counterparts, played by domestic role-players. There is also the opportunity to work through interpreters, negotiate sensitive situations, and solve problems with Afghan authorities, officials, religious leaders, and villagers, as shown in figure 5.

Figure 5: Civilian Trainees Interact with Afghan Role Players in Scenario Involving Afghan Casualties Resulting from a NATO Airstrike

Source: GAO.

Civilian-military training exercise.

State implemented internal controls to help ensure that Chief of Mission personnel took the required training before deployment. State's Office of Orientation and In-Processing acts as a central processing point for all Chief of Mission personnel deploying to Afghanistan and works with the Foreign Service Institute to ensure that all training requirements have been met. Examples of the Center's training verification activities include accessing Foreign Service Institute online registration to determine the accuracy of enrollment records, tracking completion of personnel's deployment checklists, and visiting classes to confirm enrolled personnel attended the course. According to State officials, in addition to these controls, Embassy Kabul also checks to make sure that the training requirement is met before granting country clearance to individuals about to be deployed. The Office of Orientation and In-Processing also reviews these country clearances before allowing individuals to deploy.

To test the reliability of State's internal controls, we compared State, USAID, and USDA names from a March 2011 run of ACPTS personnel data against Foreign Service Institute training records and State training waiver logs. The analysis yielded 134 names of personnel who could have potentially missed required Foreign Service Institute training. After the names were submitted to the Orientation and In-Processing Center, State stated it was able to account for all of the personnel, either by verifying that they had taken the training or possessed a valid reason for not having taken the training.[33]

According to State officials, the Office of Orientation and In-Processing and Embassy Kabul also check to verify that personnel have taken the FACT course before being deployed to Afghanistan. In June 2011, we reported that Diplomatic Security had difficulty verifying training taken by non-State personnel and made several recommendations.[34] Diplomatic Security was aware of this problem and, in June 2011, was in the process of implementing the FACT Tracker to address it. This tracker could be checked by regional security officers at high-threat posts to confirm required training was taken before granting personnel country clearance. At the time of our review, Diplomatic Security officials stated that the FACT Tracker was fully operational and could verify FACT training going back to 2005.

To test this internal control, we selected a random sample of 65 names from the July 2011 ACPTS personnel data and compared these names

---

[33]Examples included equivalent training courses taken, as well as miscellaneous approved exceptions due to inaccuracies in the March 2011 ACPTS data, such as duplicate or misspelled names and inaccurate location information. Four USAID personnel did not take required training, three of whom deployed just as the training requirement was coming into effect.

[34]For example, we recommended that Diplomatic Security develop or improve the process to track its individual training requirements and completion of training more broadly. See GAO, Diplomatic Security: *Expanded Missions and Inadequate Facilities Pose Critical Challenges to Training Efforts,* GAO-11-460 (Washington D.C.: June 1, 2011). As of October 2011, Diplomatic Security was taking steps to improve its tracking of training through collaboration with the Foreign Service Institute.

against data in the FACT Tracker. We and Diplomatic Security, through the use of the FACT Tracker, were able to account for all 65 names. As 100 percent of our sample received FACT or other appropriate training, we believe that State has established an effective system of internal controls over its training.[35]

DOD Provided Afghanistan-Specific Training to Civilians, but Some Training Contained Gaps or Duplication

According to DOD guidance, the Office of the Secretary of Defense for Personnel and Readiness is to develop policies, plans, and programs for the training of DOD personnel, including civilians.[36] In November 2010, the Office of the Secretary of Defense established counterinsurgency standards and required training of individuals and units, including DOD civilians deploying to Afghanistan, on such things as language and cultural awareness. DOD guidance also requires U.S. Central Command to coordinate and approve training necessary to carry out missions assigned to the command and U.S. Central Command-established theater-training requirements that apply to DOD civilians deployed to the command's area of responsibility.[37] U.S. Central Command theater-training requirements include general requirements such as anti-terrorism awareness training; chemical, biological, radiological, and nuclear personnel protective measures and survival skills; mine and unexploded ordnance awareness; and requirements specific to the country of deployment—for Afghanistan, the requirements include, for example, language and cultural awareness training, implementation of the Secretary of Defense-approved counterinsurgency qualification standards, and High Mobility Multipurpose Wheeled Vehicle (HMMWV) and Mine Resistant Ambush Protected (MRAP) egress training. Finally, DOD's 2010 strategic plan calls for the establishment of a requirements

---

[35]In statistical terms, given that 100 percent of our sample took FACT or other equivalent training, we can state with 95 percent confidence that fewer than about 5 percent of State, USAID, and USDA personnel in Afghanistan during July 2011 did not receive FACT training.

[36]DOD Directive 5100.01, *Functions of the Department of Defense and Its Major Components* (Dec. 21, 2010) and Department of Defense Directive 5124.02, *Under Secretary of Defense for Personnel and Readiness (USD (P&R))* (June 23, 2008). The Under Secretary of Defense for Intelligence retains oversight and policy responsibility for DOD intelligence and security components.

[37]DOD Directive 5100.01, *Functions of the Department of Defense and Its Major Components* (Dec. 21, 2010).

process that includes front-end analysis and synchronizing service training programs with combatant commander requirements.[38]

As shown in table 6, several DOD organizations deploying civilians to Afghanistan provide predeployment training to address Office of the Secretary of Defense, U.S. Central Command, and their own specific requirements. To address these requirements, each of DOD's components independently developed its own training courses; however, we identified some gaps and duplication in this training. For example, Air Force civilians deploying to Afghanistan through the CEW were required to attend both Air Force and CEW predeployment training. The CEW predeployment training consists of an 11-day course that covers areas such as personal and family benefits and legal information; survival skills, including first aid; HMMWV rollover training and Counter-Improvised Explosive Device training; and language and cultural awareness skills. As a result, those Air Force civilians deploying through the CEW received training on some of the same material, such as Counter-Improvised Explosive Device training, twice prior to deployment. According to DOD officials, in November 2011, DOD began granting some waivers from the CEW training to Air Force civilians that completed Combat Airman Skills Training.[39] However, DOD officials stated not all civilians deploying to Afghanistan are required to complete this training; therefore, Air Force civilians who do not receive Combat Airman Skills Training would still be required to complete both Air Force and CEW predeployment training. Additionally, some Army civilian training did not meet the requirements established by U.S. Central Command. For example, Army civilian training at the CONUS (continental United States) Replacement Center[40] did not cover either the U.S. Central Command-required HMMWV or MRAP vehicle rollover techniques. Table 6 lists the gaps and duplication we identified.

---

[38]DOD, *Strategic Plan for the Next Generation of Training for the Department of Defense* (Sept. 23, 2010).

[39]Combat Airman Skills Training is special training provided to personnel who will be going into a hostile and uncertain environment.

[40]The CONUS Replacement Center's mission is to receive and process individual nonunit related personnel and civilians for deployment to and redeployment from the theaters of operations.

Table 6: Gaps and Duplication in Training Courses Provided to DOD Civilians Deployed to Afghanistan

	Ministry of Defense Advisors program	Civilian Expeditionary Workforce	Afghanistan Pakistan Hands	Army Corps of Engineers	Army CONUS Replacement Center	Air Force Expeditionary Force training	Navy
Gap	None identified	None identified	None identified	Topics that should have been covered to address combatant commander theater requirements: • HMMWV and MRAP egress • Nonlethal weapons	Topics that should have been covered to address combatant commander theater requirements: • Chemical, biological, radiological, nuclear • HMMWV and MRAP egress • Nonlethal weapons	None identified	None identified
Duplication	None identified	Topics duplicated by Air Force training: • Chemical, biological, radiological, nuclear[a] • Self-aid/buddy care[a] • Cultural awareness[c] • Counter improvised explosive device training[a] • Unexploded Ordnance Awareness[a] • Survival, evasion, resistance, escape[a] • Basic marksmanship, if required[d] • Law of Armed Conflict[c]	None identified	None identified	None identified	Topics duplicated by CEW training: • Chemical, biological, radiological, nuclear[a] • Self-aid/buddy care[a] • Cultural awareness[b] • Counter improvised explosive device training[a] • Unexploded Ordnance Awareness[b] • Survival, evasion, resistance, escape[b] • Basic marksmanship, if required[d] • Law of Armed Conflict[b]	None identified

Source: GAO analysis of DOD regulations, guidance, and training curricula.

[a]Denotes training that has hands-on or computer-based or classroom components.

[b]Denotes training that is computer-based.

[c]Denotes training that is classroom-based.

[d]Denotes training that is hands on.

DOD organizations have independently developed training courses leading to some gaps and duplication in the training provided because the Office of the Secretary Defense for Personnel and Readiness, which has primary responsibility for civilian personnel policy, did not have a process for identifying baseline civilian predeployment training requirements, synchronizing service-specific training programs with combatant commander and other Office of the Secretary of Defense predeployment training requirements, and coordinating the efforts of key stakeholders, such as the military services and subordinate commands. In May 2011, we recommended that DOD improve the planning and coordination of language and culture training—a component of the Office of the Secretary of Defense's counterinsurgency training.[41] In addition, during our review, an official in the Office of the Under Secretary of Defense for Personnel and Readiness stated that training standards should be established for the department and that the Office of the Secretary of Defense for Personnel and Readiness should require the services to incorporate these standards into the training the services provide.

Without a process for identifying and synchronizing requirements and coordinating efforts to implement the requirements, the Office of the Secretary of Defense cannot ensure that DOD is preparing its civilians for deployment to Afghanistan and is using training resources efficiently.

Conclusions

The U.S. civilian presence in Afghanistan and the deployment of civilians to Afghan provinces and districts remain crucial to U.S. efforts to build the capacity of the Afghan government to provide essential services to its people with limited international support. With the increased focus on deploying more U.S. civilians throughout Afghanistan comes the need for the U.S. Mission to be able to track and monitor the movement and location of its civilian staff, especially given the ongoing drawdown of U.S. troops and plans to transition lead security responsibility to the Afghan government in 2014. We are encouraged by State and DOD's efforts to improve tracking of deployed civilian personnel. Additionally, as DOD has expanded its involvement in overseas military operations worldwide, it has grown increasingly reliant on its civilian workforce to provide support to these operations. While DOD's efforts to institutionalize the CEW are

---

[41]GAO, *Military Training: Actions Needed to Improve Planning and Coordination of Army and Marine Corps Language and Culture Training*, GAO-11-456 (Washington, D.C.: May 26, 2011).

commendable, until DOD makes decisions regarding the size of the CEW and issues implementation guidance, the CEW may not be capable of supporting future overseas operations as well as departmentwide goals to strengthen and rightsize the DOD total workforce.

Furthermore, having policies and procedures in place to help ensure that U.S. civilians receive necessary training before they deploy to a high-threat working environment such as Afghanistan can enhance their safety as well as their ability to accomplish the mission. While agencies present under Chief of Mission authority benefit from a centralized set of training requirements and internal controls, DOD's civilian training process does not have the same level of oversight or centralized control. Enhancing DOD's civilian training process would provide greater synchronization of training requirements while still allowing the various components to tailor their training to mission-specific needs.

Recommendations for Executive Action

To enable DOD to make the CEW a significant portion of the civilian workforce, meet readiness goals for the CEW, and position itself to respond to future missions, we recommend that the Secretary of Defense direct the Acting Under Secretary of Defense for Personnel and Readiness to take the following two actions:

- Develop key assumptions concerning the size and composition of the emergency-essential, non-combat essential, and capability-based volunteer categories referred to in the 2009 CEW directive.

- Finalize the implementation guidance to DOD components on how to identify and designate the number and types of positions that constitute the emergency-essential, non-combat essential, and capability-based volunteer categories.

To provide a consistent approach for synchronizing predeployment training for DOD civilians, we recommend that the Secretary of Defense direct the Acting Under Secretary of Defense for Personnel and Readiness to take the following two actions:

- Establish a process to identify and approve predeployment training requirements for all DOD civilians.

- Establish a process to coordinate with key stakeholders such as the military services and subordinate commands to ensure that requirements are synchronized among and within DOD components and with departmentwide guidance.

Agency Comments and Our Evaluation

We provided a draft of this report to DOD, State, USAID, USDA, as well as the Departments of Homeland Security, Justice and the Treasury. DOD provided written comments, reprinted in their entirety in appendix II, and concurred with our four recommendations—characterizing them as supporting its current initiative to transform the CEW. Specifically,

- DOD concurred with our recommendations to (1) develop key assumptions concerning the size and composition of the emergency-essential, non-combat essential, and capability-based volunteer categories referred to in the 2009 CEW directive and (2) finalize the implementation guidance to DOD components on how to identify and designate the number and types of positions for these categories. DOD did not specify how it would implement these recommendations.

- DOD concurred with our recommendation to establish a process to identify and approve pre-deployment training requirements for all DOD civilians. DOD stated that through the process of identifying pre-deployment training requirements, DOD will establish a core set of training needs that are applicable under all circumstances under which DOD civilians may deploy. DOD also stated that it will develop policy that recognizes the agility necessary to prepare DOD civilians for unique mission requirements and conditions now and in the future.

- DOD concurred with our recommendation to establish a process to coordinate with key stakeholders such as the military services and subordinate commands to ensure that training requirements are synchronized among and within DOD components and with department-wide guidance. DOD stated the process it develops for identifying pre-deployment training requirements will account for the need to make the best use of resources using guiding principles and criteria from the Secretary of Defense and advice from the Chairman of the Joint Chiefs of Staff as needed to ensure an agile and effective contingency workforce.

State, the Department of the Treasury, and the Department of Homeland Security provided technical comments, which we have incorporated into the report as appropriate. The Department of the Treasury noted that State's database had not been updated to reflect 13 total approved Treasury positions. Treasury further noted that two of its positions listed as "open" remained programmatically on hold, resulting in 11 active slots filled. We incorporated this technical comment in our report.

We are sending copies of this report to the appropriate congressional committees; the Secretaries of Agriculture, Defense, Homeland Security, and State; the U.S. Attorney General; the Administrator of USAID; and other interested parties. The report also is available at no charge on the GAO website at http://www.gao.gov.

If you or your staff have any questions about this report, please contact Brenda S. Farrell at (202) 512-3604 or farrellb@gao.gov or Charles Michael Johnson Jr. at (202) 512-7331 or johnsoncm@gao.gov. Contact points for our Offices of Congressional Relations and Public Affairs may be found on the last page of this report. Key contributors to this report are listed in appendix III.

Brenda S. Farrell
Director
Defense Capabilities and Management

Charles Michael Johnson Jr.
Director
International Affairs and Trade

List of Addressees

The Honorable Carl Levin
Chairman
The Honorable John McCain
Ranking Member
Committee on Armed Services
United States Senate

The Honorable John Kerry
Chairman
The Honorable Richard G. Lugar
Ranking Member
Committee on Foreign Relations
United States Senate

The Honorable Joseph I. Lieberman
Chairman
Committee on Homeland Security
   and Governmental Affairs
United States Senate

The Honorable Daniel K. Inouye
Chairman
The Honorable Thad Cochran
Ranking Member
Subcommittee on Defense
Committee on Appropriations
United States Senate

The Honorable Patrick J. Leahy
Chairman
The Honorable Lindsey Graham
Ranking Member
Subcommittee on the Department of State,
   Foreign Operations and Related Programs
Committee on Appropriations
United States Senate

The Honorable Howard P. "Buck" McKeon
Chairman
The Honorable Adam Smith
Ranking Member
Committee on Armed Services
House of Representatives

The Honorable Ileana Ros-Lehtinen
Chairman
The Honorable Howard L. Berman
Ranking Member
Committee on Foreign Affairs
House of Representatives

The Honorable C.W. Bill Young
Chairman
The Honorable Norman D. Dicks
Ranking Member
Subcommittee on Defense
Committee on Appropriations
House of Representatives

The Honorable Kay Granger
Chairwoman
The Honorable Nita M. Lowey
Ranking Member
Subcommittee on State, Foreign Operations
  and Related Programs
Committee on Appropriations
House of Representatives

The Honorable Jason Chaffetz
Chairman
The Honorable John F. Tierney
Ranking Member
Subcommittee on National Security, Homeland
  Defense and Foreign Operations
Committee on Oversight and Government Reform
House of Representatives

Appendix I: Scope and Methodology

To review the U.S. civilian presence in Afghanistan, we obtained information from pertinent strategic planning, recruitment, staffing, and reporting documents and interviewed relevant officials from the Departments of Agriculture (USDA), Defense (DOD), Homeland Security, Justice, State (State), and the Treasury, as well as the U.S. Agency for International Development (USAID). We did not examine costs for the deployment or support of civilian personnel in Afghanistan due to a concurrent review by the Office of the Special Inspector General for Afghanistan Reconstruction on this topic, published in September 2011.[1]

To examine the expansion of the U.S. civilian presence in Afghanistan, we obtained and analyzed staffing data from State and DOD regarding staffing requirements and fill rates for all civilian positions under Chief of Mission authority and key positions under combatant commander authority deployed in-country following the President's March 2009 call to enhance support of Afghan national and subnational government institutions. Our scope was limited to U.S. direct hires and did not include locally engaged staff or contractors. Because, according to DOD officials, the majority of DOD civilians directly serve in combat support positions, we focused our request for staffing data on organizations or programs intended to enhance the capacity of the Afghan government, which included the Ministry of Defense Advisors and Afghanistan Pakistan Hands programs. We validated reports on Chief of Mission staffing progress through interviews with officials representing agencies that deployed staff to fill positions in Afghanistan since January 2009, including officials from Homeland Security, Justice, State, the Treasury, USAID, and USDA. We did not meet with officials from several agencies with fewer than five permanent staff deployed to Afghanistan, such as the Departments of Transportation and Health and Human Services.

To assess the reliability of the staffing data reported by State and DOD for civilians in Afghanistan, we reviewed available documentation, examined the data for outliers and missing observations, and conducted follow-up interviews to discuss questions that arose in our analysis of the data. Additionally, for Chief of Mission data, we compared complementary datasets from State's Afghanistan Civilian Personnel Tracking System

---

[1]*The U.S. Civilian Uplift in Afghanistan Has Cost Nearly $2 Billion, and State Should Continue to Strengthen Its Management and Oversight of the Funds Transferred to Other Agencies*, Office of the Special Inspector General for Afghanistan Reconstruction Audit-11-17 and Department of State Office of Inspector General AUD/SI-11-45 (Sept. 8, 2011).

(ACPTS) and the Chief of Mission Civilian Staffing Matrix to identify whether any reporting discrepancies existed. We requested datasets from State from each database over corresponding time periods; our first data run compared February 10, 2011, Chief of Mission Civilian Staffing data with March 16, 2011, ACPTS data; our second data run compared June 28, 2011, Chief of Mission Civilian Staffing Matrix data with July 7, 2011, ACPTS data. We further met with State officials to identify the cause and effect of discrepancies that were found to exist, in order to assess whether the discrepancies limit the ability of U.S. agencies to evaluate their staffing progress. For DOD, we requested data from the Ministry of Defense Advisors program, the Afghanistan Pakistan Hands program, and the Joint Personnel Status Report to identify DOD's civilian presence in Afghanistan. We also met with officials from the Ministry of Defense Advisors program, Afghanistan Pakistan Hands program, and Joint Chiefs of Staff to discuss the data sources, internal controls, and data reliability related to their respective staffing data. We found State civilian staffing data for Afghanistan to be sufficiently reliable to provide an indication of the positions filled at the level of the agency, but State ACPTS data were not sufficiently reliable to report on more-detailed staffing information, such as position type. For the Ministry of Defense Advisors program and the Afghanistan Pakistan Hands program, we found that program documents supported the requirements and the number of filled positions that the program offices provided and that the data from these programs were sufficiently reliable to illustrate the positions filled within these programs. However, the extent to which DOD staffing data in the Joint Personnel Status Report are reliable is unknown because previous reports have omitted or double counted personnel. DOD officials noted that while errors do occur in the daily submission of Joint Personnel Status Report data from the combatant commands, the reports are accurate enough to identify trends in DOD's civilian presence over time, and we agree. As of late 2011, we could not fully verify the accuracy of the ACPTS system. However, during the course of our review and after several discussions with us regarding data reliability, State began taking steps to improve the reliability of the ACPTS database.

To evaluate the implementation of DOD's Civilian Expeditionary Workforce (CEW) policy, we obtained and reviewed relevant documents. Specifically, we reviewed the DOD directive that established the program to understand the structure of the CEW as presented in this document and reviewed the 2009 DOD Civilian Human Capital Strategic Plan to identify the steps DOD had established as a road map for implementing the CEW directive. We also reviewed other documents such as DOD's Strategic Management Plan Fiscal Years 2012-2013 to determine how the CEW related to high-priority departmentwide programs. In addition, we interviewed Office of the Secretary of Defense and CEW program officials to further understand the current status of efforts to fully implement the CEW and the department's plans for the CEW of the future. We also interviewed U.S. Central Command officials to determine how the CEW was being used to satisfy its needs for deployable civilians in Afghanistan and officials from the Air Force, Army, and Navy, to determine how these agencies coordinated efforts to identify deployable civilians.

To determine the extent to which U.S. agencies had provided required Afghanistan-specific training to their personnel before deployment, we reviewed predeployment training requirements established by the Department of State for all Chief of Mission personnel and the requirements set by various programs and components within the DOD. We did not analyze training provided by the Department of Justice or its components due to its specialized law-enforcement nature. For DOD training, we reviewed training programs for the CEW, Ministry of Defense Advisors program, Afghanistan Pakistan Hands program, and U.S. Army Corps of Engineers as well as civilian training for the Air Force, Army, and Navy. We focused on these DOD programs because of their capacity-building focus. On two separate occasions, we observed scenario-based training administered to Chief of Mission personnel and the Ministry of Defense Advisors program, both held at the Muscatatuck Urban Training Center in Indiana.

To assess the extent to which the agencies complied with predeployment training requirements for Chief of Mission personnel, we compared a March 2011 data run of State, USAID, and USDA personnel from State's ACPTS system against Foreign Service Institute training rosters for the three Afghanistan-specific, mandatory training courses as well as against a State training waiver log. We focused on State, USAID, and USDA personnel due to the size of their respective civilian presence, as well as their primacy in deploying civilians to the field. This analysis yielded 134 names that did not appear on the Foreign Service Institute rosters or in the waiver log, which we submitted to State's Office of Orientation and In-Processing for explanation. Additionally, to test Diplomatic Security's FACT Tracker, we selected a random sample of 65 State, USAID, and USDA names from July 2011 ACPTS personnel data and compared these names against data in the FACT Tracker. This sample was designed so that if we found that all sample cases received FACT or other appropriate training, we would be at least 95 percent confident that fewer than about 5 percent of State, USAID, and USDA personnel in

Afghanistan during July 2011 did not receive FACT training. Although we note weaknesses in ACPTS's data reliability, we judged the database sufficiently reliable to compare names against training rosters, waiver logs, and the FACT Tracker.

For DOD personnel, we compared the training curricula utilized by the military services, defense agencies, and the CEW to U.S. Central Command, U.S. Forces—Afghanistan, and Office of the Secretary of Defense requirements and guidance to see whether the training addressed the requirements. In addition, we compared the various training received by deploying civilians to determine if there was any duplication or repetition in the training provided. Because training record keeping within DOD is decentralized, we did not verify individual training records to establish whether deployed civilians had received the required training. We did, however, review the procedures that the military services and defense agencies have in place to ensure that deploying civilians have taken required training. In addition, we interviewed officials with the Office of the Under Secretary of Defense for Personnel and Readiness, CEW training office, Air Force, Army, Navy, U.S. Army Corps of Engineers, and U.S. Central Command to discuss the predeployment training requirements for deployed civilians.

We conducted this performance audit from May 2010 to February 2012 in accordance with generally accepted government auditing standards. Those standards require that we plan and perform the audit to obtain sufficient, appropriate evidence to provide a reasonable basis for our findings and conclusions based on our audit objectives. We believe that the evidence obtained provides a reasonable basis for our findings and conclusions based on our audit objectives.

Appendix II: Comments from the Department of Defense

OFFICE OF THE UNDER SECRETARY OF DEFENSE
4000 DEFENSE PENTAGON
WASHINGTON, D.C. 20301-4000

FEB 15 2012

PERSONNEL AND
READINESS

Ms. Brenda S. Farrell
Director, Defense Capabilities and Management
U.S. Government Accountability Office
441 G Street, NW
Washington DC 20548

Dear Ms. Farrell:

     Enclosed is the Department of Defense (DoD) response to the GAO Draft Report, GAO-12-285, "AFGHANISTAN: Improvements Needed to Strengthen Management of U.S. Civilian Presence," dated February 2012 (GAO Code 320766). We believe your thoughtful recommendations support our current initiative to transform the Civilian Expeditionary Workforce Program.

     Please feel free to contact, Mr. John Moseley, our primary action officer for this report at (703) 696-5375 for additional information.

Sincerely,

P.M. Tamburrino, Jr.
Deputy Assistant Secretary
Civilian Personnel Policy

Enclosure:
As stated

GAO DRAFT REPORT DATED FEBRUARY 2012
GAO-12-285 (GAO CODE 320766)

"AFGHANISTAN: IMPROVEMENTS NEEDED TO STRENGTHEN
MANAGEMENT OF U.S. CIVILIAN PRESENCE"

DEPARTMENT OF DEFENSE COMMENTS
TO THE GAO RECOMMENDATIONS AND REPORT COMMENTS

RECOMMENDATION 1: The GAO recommends that the Secretary of Defense direct the Under Secretary of Defense for Personnel and Readiness to develop key assumptions concerning the size and composition of the emergency-essential, non-combat essential, and capability-based volunteer categories referred to in the 2009 CEW directive.

DoD RESPONSE: Concur.

RECOMMENDATION 2: The GAO recommends that the Secretary of Defense direct the Under Secretary of Defense for Personnel and Readiness to finalize the implementation guidance to DOD components on how to identify and designate the number and types of positions that comprise the emergency-essential, non-combat essential, and capability-based volunteer categories.

DoD RESPONSE: Concur.

RECOMMENDATION 3: The GAO recommends that the Secretary of Defense direct the Under Secretary of Defense for Personnel and Readiness to establish a process to identify and approve pre-deployment training requirements for all DOD civilians.

DoD RESPONSE: Concur. Currently, DoD civilians deploy under at least four different circumstances: 1) to support the mission requirements of an individual Component, 2) to support an overarching Department of Defense mission, 3) to support a joint requirement driven by a Combatant Command, or 4) on a limited basis to support the mission of another Federal agency. Through the process of identifying pre-deployment training requirements, DoD will establish a core set of training needs that are applicable under all circumstances along with policy that recognizes the agility necessary to prepare DoD civilians for unique mission requirements and conditions now and in the future.

2

RECOMMENDATION 4: The GAO recommends that the Secretary of Defense direct the Under Secretary of Defense for Personnel and Readiness to establish a process to coordinate with key stakeholders such as the military services and subordinate commands to ensure that requirements are synchronized among and within DOD components and with the department-wide guidance.

DoD RESPONSE: Concur. The process will account for the need to make the best use of resources using guiding principles and criteria from the Secretary of Defense and advice from the Chairman of the Joint Chiefs of Staff as needed to ensure an agile and effective contingency workforce.

COMMENT: Reference page 31, paragraph 2. Current sources in AFCENT state that Air Force deployees attend only AF training. In the spirit and intent of this report, the Department will ensure appropriate training is based on the assignment and location of deployment and ensure the best use of pre-deployment training sources to achieve optimum economies of scale.

Appendix III: GAO Contacts and Staff Acknowledgments

GAO Contacts	Brenda S. Farrell, (202) 512-3604 or farrellb@gao.gov Charles Michael Johnson Jr., (202) 512-7331 or johnsoncm@gao.gov
Staff Acknowledgments	In addition to the contacts named above, Hynek Kalkus, Assistant Director; Kimberly Seay, Assistant Director; David Adams; Adam Bonnifield; Virginia Chanley; David Hancock; Mae Jones; Linda Keefer; Shakira O'Neil; and John Wren made key contributions to this report.

GAO's Mission	The Government Accountability Office, the audit, evaluation, and investigative arm of Congress, exists to support Congress in meeting its constitutional responsibilities and to help improve the performance and accountability of the federal government for the American people. GAO examines the use of public funds; evaluates federal programs and policies; and provides analyses, recommendations, and other assistance to help Congress make informed oversight, policy, and funding decisions. GAO's commitment to good government is reflected in its core values of accountability, integrity, and reliability.
Obtaining Copies of GAO Reports and Testimony	The fastest and easiest way to obtain copies of GAO documents at no cost is through GAO's website (www.gao.gov). Each weekday afternoon, GAO posts on its website newly released reports, testimony, and correspondence. To have GAO e-mail you a list of newly posted products, go to www.gao.gov and select "E-mail Updates."
Order by Phone	The price of each GAO publication reflects GAO's actual cost of production and distribution and depends on the number of pages in the publication and whether the publication is printed in color or black and white. Pricing and ordering information is posted on GAO's website, http://www.gao.gov/ordering.htm. Place orders by calling (202) 512-6000, toll free (866) 801-7077, or TDD (202) 512-2537. Orders may be paid for using American Express, Discover Card, MasterCard, Visa, check, or money order. Call for additional information.
Connect with GAO	Connect with GAO on Facebook, Flickr, Twitter, and YouTube. Subscribe to our RSS Feeds or E-mail Updates. Listen to our Podcasts. Visit GAO on the web at www.gao.gov.
To Report Fraud, Waste, and Abuse in Federal Programs	Contact: Website: www.gao.gov/fraudnet/fraudnet.htm E-mail: fraudnet@gao.gov Automated answering system: (800) 424-5454 or (202) 512-7470
Congressional Relations	Katherine Siggerud, Managing Director, siggerudk@gao.gov, (202) 512-4400, U.S. Government Accountability Office, 441 G Street NW, Room 7125, Washington, DC 20548
Public Affairs	Chuck Young, Managing Director, youngc1@gao.gov, (202) 512-4800 U.S. Government Accountability Office, 441 G Street NW, Room 7149 Washington, DC 20548

Please Print on Recycled Paper.